Green Investing
How to Align Your Finances with Your Eco-Conscious Values

Table of Contents

Chapter 1. Introduction

Welcome to this Special Report that is set to be your guiding light in your journey to aligning your financial investments with your steadfast eco-conscious values! Get ready to navigate the thrilling world of green investing, a sphere that proves it's not only possible but also highly fruitful to put your money where your heart is. This comprehensive report includes easy-to-understand guides, viable green investment options, plus tips, case studies, interviews from industry experts, and more. You'll emerge not only with a richer understanding but also concrete strategies to help your finances grow 'greener'. So let's dive in, and make your money a powerful force for global environmental sustainability!

Chapter 2. Understanding Green Investing: An Introduction

Green investing, also referred to as "sustainable", "socially responsible", or "impact" investing, encapsulates a wide range of investment approaches that seek not just monetary returns but also a positive environmental impact. The philosophy behind green investing is pretty simple: invest in companies that contribute or aim to contribute to environmental solutions, while avoiding those that either have negative impacts on the environment or remain indifferent to environmental issues.

2.1. The Genesis of Green Investing

A look back at history shows that green investing originated from the broader concept of socially responsible investing (SRI), which began in the 1960s. The SRI movement evolved from an aversion to investing in firms participating in undesirable activities such as tobacco, firearms, and apartheid South Africa. With time, this philosophy of 'avoidance' broadened into 'positive investing'—a proactive approach of making financial commitments in businesses that bring about societal good.

During the 1990s and early 2000s, particular emphasis began to be placed on environmental issues—marking the birth of green investing. Today, green investing has evolved into an influential part of the modern investment landscape. It increasingly attracts individuals and institutions wishing to express their environmental concerns through their investment choices.

2.2. Identifying Green Investments

Green investing most commonly pertains to the direct or indirect funding of companies or projects that are committed to conserving natural resources, implementing clean air and water projects, or reducing emissions and waste. Some examples include green bonds, mutual funds focused on environmentally responsible companies, direct investments in renewable energy projects, and exchange-traded funds (ETFs) focused on clean technology.

Yet identifying truly green investments isn't always straightforward. This is due, in part, to the absence of a universally accepted definition of what sustainability implies. You might encounter terms such as "Environmental, Social, and Governance" (ESG), "green", "sustainable", and "impact" used interchangeably, yet their interpretations could vary significantly. However, all are directed towards a common goal of creating long-term stakeholder value through an integration of economic, environmental, and ethical considerations.

2.3. Understanding Greenwashing

Investors need to be aware of 'greenwashing', a form of marketing spin where a company or government body presents itself as environmentally friendly when its practices say otherwise. Greenwashed products may verbally or visually suggest a product is 'green' or environmentally friendly, whereas the actual impact may be negligible or even negative. Dishonest practice can mislead investors about the environmental benefits of an investment, and may result in investors unwittingly supporting companies and practices that don't align with their environmental values.

2.4. Measuring and Managing Environmental Impact

A critical piece of the green investment process is determining and managing the environmental impact. For a more holistic look at a company's performance, investors now look beyond traditional financial metrics and incorporate ESG metrics into their analysis. ESG metrics provide insights into a company's environmental impact, its relationships with stakeholders, and its management structure. However, quantifying environmental impact isn't straightforward. There is currently no single, standardized approach to measure it. Rather, myriad third-party rating and scoring systems exist, presenting some challenges for investors in comparing investments or creating a diversified portfolio.

2.5. The Future of Green Investing

Green investing is at the cusp of a transformative era as an increasing number of investors are aiming to align their investments with their values. This shift is largely driven by heightened awareness of the immense challenges our planet faces in the form of climate change, pollution, and resource scarcity, among others. Furthermore, advancements in technology are making it easier for investors to assess the sustainability and environmental impact of their investments, fostering transparency and accountability. It's becoming more possible, and increasingly necessary, to secure financial returns while also promoting environmental sustainability.

Perhaps most excitingly, as the scale of green investing grows, there's potential for it to spur significant innovation and transformation within industries. After all, where capital goes, innovation often follows. As businesses increasingly recognize that sustainability can drive value, and as investors vote with their wallets, we can expect to see more companies making tangible, impactful commitments to environmental practices.

Throughout this report, we will provide a practical guide to exploring the world of green investing in depth, helping you make informed decisions that don't compromise your financial goals or your commitment to the environment.

Making the switch to green investing might require an initial leap of faith, but it's a leap that leads towards a more sustainable and prosperous world for everyone.

Chapter 3. The Environmental Impact: Our Role and Responsibility

Climate change, fuelled by human activities, is upon us. Rising global temperatures, melting ice caps, forest fires, and extreme weather events, are stark reminders of our environmental responsibilities and the urgency to transition towards sustainable practices. As an investor, you carry an influential role in driving this transformation.

3.1. The Reality & Urgency of Environmental Issues

Our planet is currently witnessing an acceleration of environmental crises. The Intergovernmental Panel on Climate Change (IPCC) highlights that the global temperature increase needs to remain under 1.5 degrees Celsius to avoid catastrophic environmental impacts. This objective requires a reduction in global greenhouse gas emission by 45% from 2010 levels by 2030 and to reach net-zero emissions by 2050.

Moreover, there's an escalating crisis of biodiversity loss. The IPBES Global Assessment Report on Biodiversity and Ecosystem Services revealed that human actions have significantly altered 75% of the earth's land and 66% of the marine environment. An astounding one million species (out of an estimated eight million) currently face extinction, many within decades.

Such statistics indicate an urgent need for change. As an investor, understanding and acknowledging this urgency is your first step towards shouldering environmental responsibility.

3.2. The Environmental Footprint of Investment

Often overlooked is the environmental footprint of our investments. The finance sector, a major force steering world economy, possesses the power to influence the trajectory of environmental sustainability. But how does our investment have an environmental footprint?

Companies utilise finance to scale their operations. If these operations are detrimental to the environment (over-exploitation of resources, carbon-intensive practices), the financial backing indirectly contributes to the environmental harm. As an investor, therefore, your investment could unwittingly support detrimental activities.

Conversely, by placing your investments in companies following sustainable practices, you bolster their operations, enabling the green economy's growth.

3.3. Investor's Role in Boosting Green Economy

Shifting investments toward companies engaged in environmental conservation and innovative technology can help drive the worldwide transition towards sustainability. In sectors from energy to manufacturing and real estate, your investment can fund the development and commercialisation of green technologies, fostering carbon-neutral industries and consumption patterns.

This financial reorientation not only contributes to the fight against climate change and biodiversity loss but could also provide substantial economic benefits. According to a report by the Global Commission on Economy and Climate, a shift to a low-carbon, sustainable growth path could deliver at least $26 trillion in economic benefits through 2030.

Thus, your role as an investor can be pivotal in the transition to green economies, helping align global growth with environmental sustainability.

3.4. The Stewardship Principle

The Stewardship Principle in investing furthers the idea of active ownership, where you, as an investor, use your position to influence a company's direction positively. This might involve voting on corporate resolutions, engaging in dialogues with management, or participating in shareholder activism initiatives focusing on environmental concerns.

Through stewardship, you can push for more responsible corporate conduct, demanding greater transparency and accountability on environmental risks and impacts.

3.5. The Role of Diversity and Inclusion

Beyond climate change, an ecologically sustainable world also focuses on social factors, including diversity and inclusion. Studies show that diverse groups often make better decisions, are more innovative, and have better risk management.

Companies that incorporate diversity in their decision-making process are likely to confer a broader spectrum of perspectives and solutions to environmental issues. Thus, investing in companies promoting diversity could have indirect positive environmental implications.

Moreover, incorporating diversity and inclusion principles in your investment strategy ties in with the broader concept of sustainable development – balancing social, environmental, and economic needs.

3.6. Responsible Investing: Our Key Responsibility

The scale and complexity of environmental challenges require significant financial resources. Having recognized our influential role as investors in facilitating an environmental transition, it is essential to adopt Responsible Investing (RI) principles.

RI integrates Environmental, Social, and Governance (ESG) factors into investment decisions. ESG-centric investing allows us to support sustainability-focused businesses and hold them accountable for their environmental impacts, driving a transition to a low-carbon and resource-efficient world.

In conclusion, as investors in this critical juncture of environmental crises, we play a key role in shaping our planet's future. Upholding our environmental responsibilities involves educating ourselves on sustainability issues and embodying the principles of responsible investing. Let's make our investments a force for environmental good, fostering the birth of a sustainable world.

Chapter 4. Demystifying the Green Finance Market Landscape

The green finance market landscape is a broad ecosystem spanning various components. As such, we will systematically cover its key aspects in this discussion, taking you through its various stages - introduction, scope, benefits, instruments, types, and also some of the challenges it faces.

4.1. The Genesis of Green Finance

Green finance emerged from the growing global concern about climate change and its profound impacts on the environment, economy, and society. The mounting evidence of anthropogenic climate change and the urgent need for solutions drove the emergence of financial mechanisms and markets that prioritize environmental sustainability.

As an instrument of sustainable development, green finance represents a paradigm shift in the financial market - integrating environmental, social, and governance (ESG) concerns into investment decisions. It acknowledges that finance has a critical role to play in addressing environmental issues and facilitating the transition to a low-carbon economy.

4.2. The Scope of Green Finance

Green finance encompasses a broad range of financial instruments and services, including green bonds and loans, green investment funds, and green insurance. It covers all financial movements aimed at benefiting the environment, either directly or indirectly. It is a gateway to the broader field of sustainable financing, which also includes economic and social factors.

Moreover, green finance is not limited to a particular sector. It permeates all industries and areas of the economy, from renewable energy and green construction to tourism, agriculture, and transportation. Essentially, any sector can become a habitable landscape for green finance, given it meets the eco-friendly objectives.

4.3. The Benefits of Green Finance

Green finance offers several benefits, reflecting its dual objective of generating financial returns and promoting sustainability.

Firstly, green finance can provide new investment opportunities. As countries and companies worldwide transition to sustainable practices, they require significant funding, opening new investment avenues.

Secondly, green finance can reduce risk. Investments that take into account environmental risks are generally more resilient to changing policy landscapes, market disruptions, and physical risks associated with climate change.

Finally, green finance can generate positive environmental impacts. By channeling capital towards sustainable projects, green finance can contribute to climate change mitigation and adaptation, biodiversity preservation, and other environmental goals.

4.4. Green Finance Instruments

There are several key instruments that facilitate green finance:

1. Green Bonds: This debt instrument is issued by corporations, municipalities, or other entities to raise capital for green projects.

They are evaluated by third parties to ensure compliance with environmental standards.

2. Green Loans: These are loan facilities granted for funding environmentally friendly projects. They can be offered in various forms, such as subsidies, preferential interest rates, or grants.

3. Green Funds: These are investment vehicles collecting capital from a group of investors to invest in a diversified portfolio of green projects or companies.

4. Green Insurance: This is a type of insurance that covers risks related to green investments and encourages risk mitigation.

4.5. Types of Green Finance

The green finance sector can be broadly classified into four types:

1. Public Finance: This includes government expenditures, grants, and subsidies aimed at delivering environmental benefits.

2. Private Finance: This comprises individual and institutional investments in sustainable projects and companies.

3. Project Finance: This involves the financing of long-term, capital-intensive infrastructure projects based on the projected cash flows of the specific project.

4. Carbon Finance: This is anchored on the financial benefits of reducing greenhouse gas emissions.

4.6. Challenges in Green Finance

Despite its growing popularity, green finance faces several challenges. These include a lack of standardized definitions and regulatory frameworks to assess what constitutes a 'green' investment, and limited transparency in reporting environmental impacts. Additionally, there is a significant gap between the amount of funding needed for worldwide sustainable development and the amount currently available.

Despite these challenges, there's considerable potential for growth and innovation in the green finance domain. Navigating this landscape requires an understanding of the dynamics at play as well as a keen eye for emerging opportunities. Only with a solid grasp of this market, can one make truly informed, sustainable investment decisions.

Chapter 5. Investment Strategies for the Eco-Conscious Investor

Investment strategies for the eco-conscious investor involve a careful alignment between your financial goals and deep-seated values for a sustainable environment. They require meticulous assessment and thoughtful decision-making not only to ensure the preservation of our planet but also to help your portfolio thrive.

5.1. The Green Investment Overview

Let's start with a basic understanding of green investing. Essentially, it is an investment approach that emphasizes backing companies and projects that prioritize environmental conservation.

In response to increasing awareness and urgency about environmental issues, such as climate change and global warming, more investors are directing their funds towards environmentally-friendly industries and companies. This movement towards sustainable investing can be broadly classified into sectors like clean energy, sustainable agriculture, green transport, water management, and waste reduction, which are all doing their part to mitigate environmental issues in diverse ways.

5.2. Understanding the ESG Criteria

One of the fundamental tenets of eco-conscious investing is based on ESG (Environmental, Social, and Governance) criteria, an evaluation approach that measures the sustainability and societal impact of an investment.

- **Environmental Criteria** assess how a company is managing its environmental responsibilities, which may include its carbon emissions, waste management, natural resource conservation, and treatment of animals, amongst others.

- **Social Criteria** investigate how the firm manages relationships with its employees, suppliers, customers, and the community where it operates.

- **Governance Criteria** relate to a company's leadership, executive pay, shareholder rights, audits, and internal controls.

5.3. Green Stocks

Green stocks represent companies that are focused on forwarding environmentally friendly or green technologies in their operations. Numerous markets and indexes spotlight these companies, such as the NASDAQ Clean Edge Green Energy Index or the S&P Global Clean Energy Index.

However, investing in green stocks is not without risk. While the domain seems promising, it's still relatively new compared to conventional markets. Hence, it is advisable to balance your portfolio with a diversified selection of stocks instead of going only for green ones.

5.4. Clean Energy Bonds

At this point, you may want to consider bond investments. Bonds are IOUs issued by organizations that promise to repay the borrowed money at a set interest rate by a certain date. They could be an attractive option for you, especially if you'd prefer a relatively safe and stable investment.

Clean energy bonds, usually offered by municipalities or companies, are used to finance renewable energy projects. Some are tax-exempt, which can make them even more of an attractive proposition. Remember, though, these bonds generally have longer maturity periods; thus, they require a longer-term investment plan.

5.5. Mutual Funds and ETFs

If you're thinking of tapping into the diversified investment pool, mutual funds and exchange-traded funds (ETFs) can be your go-to choices. Both options offer broad exposure to a selection of green assets, with the advantage of being managed by professional fund managers.

For example, there are a number of mutual funds focused on companies that score highly on ESG criteria. Similarly, ETFs provide exposure to a plethora of clean energy companies and industries. Notably, ETFs offer the additional flexibility of being able to be traded like stocks throughout the day.

5.6. Green Real Estate Investments

An often overlooked area of green investing is the realm of Real Estate Investment Trusts (REITs) or direct investment in properties. Green real estate emphasizes energy-efficient buildings and sustainable constructions, often lucrative due to built-in long-term power savings and consumer demand for eco-friendly dwellings.

5.7. Conclusion

Remember, in addition to aligning with your values, green investing can also be financially rewarding. By consciously directing your capital towards companies and industries that are accelerating the transition toward a sustainable future, you're doing your part in combatting climate change and other environmental challenges. As with any investment plan, though, it's important to do your research and take a balanced, diverse approach.

5.8. Further Reading

We recommend you follow up this chapter with a delve into our section on 'Green Investment Risks and Returns'. You should also check the 'Interviews with Investment Professionals' chapter for first-hand accounts and tips on successful green investing strategies. To deepen your knowledge further, have a look at the 'Case Studies' section for real life examples and illustrations. Useful appendices such as 'Sustainable Investing Glossary' and 'Must-know Green Investment Terms' are also at your disposal.

Through your journey in eco-conscious investing, always remember, your investments can truly become a powerful mechanism for positive global change!

Chapter 6. Implementing a Sustainable Financial Plan: Step-by-Step Approach

To take those first important steps towards implementing a sustainable financial plan, you'll need to align your finances with your values, invest in eco-friendly sources, and understand the impact of your investments. These systematic steps will guide you on this journey.

6.1. Understand Your Current Financial Standing and Your Eco-Conscious Goals

Firstly, reassess your current financial situation including, but not limited to your income, expenses, assets, liabilities, and investments. You'll then be better placed to understand how your current financial decisions align (or don't) with your environmental values. Ask yourself, do your current investments allow you to sleep peacefully at night knowing you are contributing positively to the environment?

Next, enumerate your eco-conscious goals. Are you aiming to significantly reduce your carbon footprint? Are you inclined towards supporting companies focused on alternative energy sources? Or are you intent on promoting sustainable agriculture? Your goals will guide your future investment decisions.

6.2. Identify Sustainable Investments That Align With Your Goals

Now that you have your goals laid out, it's time to search for sustainable investments that align with them. Sustainable investments typically focus on companies that practice environmental, social, and corporate governance (ESG) norms. Look into industries such as renewable energy, sustainable agriculture, green real estate, and impact investing. Be aware that while some may boast impressive green credentials, a thorough research of company practices and impacts will stop you falling prey to 'greenwashing'.

6.3. Screen Your Investments

Once you've pinpointed potential investments, you need to apply screening criteria. These might include the company's environmental impact, sustainability reports, and their social responsibility indices. Check their official reports, third-party assessments, and news publications to understand their environmental footprint. It's a demanding, but crucial, step to avoiding investments that might clash with your green values.

6.4. Diversify Your Investment Portfolio

Diversification is key in any investment strategy and sustainable investing is no exception. Spread your investments across various sectors, jurisdictions, and asset types that align with your eco-principles. This strategy will help you balance risks and rewards while achieving your greener financial objectives.

6.5. Get Professional Advice

Consider turning to financial advisors or investment firms that specialize in green investments. Having a professional partner with a deep understanding of sustainable finance can be invaluable in navigating this relatively new sphere. They'll give you advice on portfolio optimization, accurate screening, reporting, and disclosing practices.

6.6. Understand and Assess Investment Risks

Intrinsically tied to every investment are risks. It's critical to be aware of potential risks associated with sustainable investments: think financial, regulatory, and 'greenwashing' risks. So, analyze these and consider getting professional advice to perform in-depth risk assessments for your portfolio.

6.7. Adjust Your Plan Periodically

The world of sustainable finance is dynamic and rapidly evolving. Your financial plan must reflect this dynamism; revisiting and adjusting your plan at regular intervals ensures it remains aligned with your goals. New types of sustainable investments may emerge, existing ones may falter, and your personal financial situation may change - all factors influencing a timely review and adjustment of your plan.

Herein lies your comprehensive step-by-step guide to creating your sustainable financial plan. Remember, the way your money grows can change the world. By consciously choosing to invest in a sustainable financial plan, not only are you securing your financial future, you're also making sure that future is brighter and greener.

Now that you know these steps, the next section will guide you through some of the viable green investment options that you can consider.

Chapter 7. Creating a Balanced Green Portfolio: Tips and Tricks

Before diving into the intricate details of creating a balanced green portfolio, it is worth noting the vital position such an endeavor occupies in the grand scheme of not just your individual financial growth, but also in the wider context of global environmental sustainability. Strategically investing in environmentally-friendly companies and initiatives is not only a move toward preserving our planet, but it also represents a booming market with excellent return prospects. This chapter will guide you through the steps you need to follow to create a balanced green portfolio and share a variety of tips and tricks to help you.

7.1. Understanding Green Investment

Green investment, also known as impact or ESG (Environmental, Social, and Governance) investing, involves channelling money into businesses or projects that have a positive impact on the environment. This includes sectors like renewable energy, sustainable agriculture, green technology, etc. The goal here is to consider not just the financial returns on an investment but also its environmental, social, and governance impacts.

As the climate crisis surges, interest in green investment is increasing. Therefore, having a well-balanced green portfolio is no longer just a moral choice but a necessary strategy for risk management and for securing future financial solidity.

7.2. Building the Foundation: Goal Setting and Risk Analysis

Before you begin creating your green portfolio, you need to set your investment goals and conduct a risk analysis. Your goals, along with your risk tolerance and investment horizon, will drastically shape your green portfolio.

Start by defining what you want to achieve through your investment portfolio. Some common financial goals include retirement funds, a financial safety net, college tuition, buying a house, etc.

This step goes hand-in-hand with conducting an honest assessment of your risk tolerance. Are you comfortable investing mostly in stocks, which can be volatile but generally offer a higher return in the long term, or do you prefer more stable, lower-risk assets like bonds? Understanding your investment comfort zone is crucial for building a green portfolio that suits your financial temperament.

7.3. Research and Selection of Green Assets

Once you have a clear understanding of your goals, risk tolerance, and investment horizon, you can start researching potential green assets. This will form the backbone of your green investment portfolio.

The universe of green assets is broad and growing rapidly. You can invest in green bonds issued by governments and companies to finance environmentally-friendly projects, stocks of companies operating in the renewable energy sector, Exchange Traded Funds (ETFs) and mutual funds targeting ESG criteria, to name a few.

A careful due diligence is required for this step. Check the company's impact reports to gauge how deeply ingrained the ESG principles are in the company's operation. Assets with high green ratings are a good place to start. However, remember to diversify within green sectors to spread out risk.

7.4. Portfolio Construction and Diversification

With a strong selection of green assets at your disposal, the next step is constructing your portfolio. A critical aspect of this construction is diversification.

Diversification is the essence of managing risk in your portfolio. An ideal green portfolio should be diversified across items such as asset class, geographical location, and industry sector. This ensures that the portfolio is not overwhelmingly affected by the financial downturn in any one area.

For example, your green portfolio might include green bonds from different sectors (technology, transport, energy), ETFs with different geographical focuses, and direct stocks from various green companies. This effectively mitigates risk and opens up opportunities for higher returns.

7.5. Regular Monitoring and Rebalancing

Once your green portfolio is established, you need to regularly monitor and rebalance it. The value of your different investments will fluctuate, so regular check-ins will help you maintain the optimal weightings you originally envisioned for your portfolio.

This might require occasional buying and selling. Perhaps one asset class has performed exceptionally well, pushing your portfolio's balance beyond your original allocation toward high risk. In this case, selling some of that asset and redirecting it towards more stable investments might be needed.

7.6. Conclusion

Creating a balanced green portfolio is a sustainable and economically rewarding financial strategy. By understanding green investment, setting your goals and risk tolerance, doing your homework on green assets, diversifying your investments, and conducting regular asset reviews, you can build a green portfolio that's both financially robust and eco-friendly.

Remember that the information provided here is to get you started; green investing can be a complex field, which may require consultation with a financial adviser. However, with the right research, commitment, and patience, creating a balanced green portfolio can be an exciting and rewarding endeavour in your journey to achieve financial growth and environmental sustainability.

Chapter 8. Exploring Green Bonds, ETFs and Mutual Funds

Green bonds, ETFs, and mutual funds are some of the most notable instruments for green investing. Before you can successfully navigate these waters, understanding the fundamentals is pivotal. Let's start by breaking down each of these investment tools on an individual level.

8.1. Understanding Green Bonds

Green Bonds are debt securities issued by corporations or governments to raise capital expressly to fund projects with eco-friendly or climate benefits. In essence, when you buy a green bond, you're lending money to the issuer for a 'green' cause, such as clean energy, sustainable transport, or biodiversity conservation.

The use of proceeds from green bonds is intentionally allocated to these environmentally-friendly projects, offering you, the investor, a chance to purposefully channel your funds to support sustainability while simultaneously earning interest on your investment.

8.2. Why Consider Green Bonds

The allure of green bonds lies not only in their environmental impact but also in their strategic financial benefits. They can offer competitive returns, especially considering the growing global focus and regulatory support for sustainable projects. Further, green bonds have shown resilience in downturn markets, often maintaining stability as compared to traditional bonds.

However, it's essential to evaluate the issuer's credibility and commitment to the promised 'green' project for the integrity of your investment and its intended impact.

8.3. Green Bonds – A Closer Look at Risk and Return

Green Bonds are not exempt from risks. They indeed face market, credit, and interest rate risks akin to conventional bonds. Some green bonds might also face potential greenwashing – a practice where projects are mislabeld as 'green'. Regulatory bodies and independent third-party rating systems help mitigate such threats. Moreover, green bonds may exhibit slightly lower liquidity compared to traditional bonds.

For returns, green bonds often yield comparable returns to traditional bonds, making them a viable choice for investors looking to combine financial returns with thorough environmental commitment.

8.4. Understanding ETFs and Mutual Funds

Exchange Traded Funds (ETFs) and Mutual Funds are excellent investment tools that allow investors to pool their money together to invest in a diversified portfolio of assets. These could include stocks, bonds, and other securities.

Green ETFs and Mutual Funds, therefore, incorporate ESG (Environmental, Social, and Governance) metrics or focus on industries that are eco-friendly. They give investors the chance to support companies that are socially responsible and contribute to a healthier planet.

8.5. Green ETFs – Why They Matter

Green ETFs provide a cost-effective and liquid way to invest in environmentally-friendly sectors. As an investor, you can purchase and sell ETF shares on an exchange just like any other public stock, providing flexibility and ease of access.

Having a diversified portfolio of numerous green companies through an ETF helps spread out and manage risk. As some sectors can be volatile, it's advantageous to have investments spread across different industries and regions.

=== Green ETFs – Scrutinizing Risk and Return

As with any other investment, green ETFs have their inherent risks. Market volatility can drastically affect returns, and the still-emerging nature of many 'green' sectors can entail further uncertainty.

However, green ETFs usually ensure a level of diversification, which can limit exposure to these risks. And with the rising global focus on sustainability, green ETFs offer immense potential for high returns, making them an attractive investment choice for the eco-conscious investor.

8.6. Green Mutual Funds – An Ideal Pick?

Green Mutual Funds let you invest in a basket of stocks or bonds from companies that maintain robust environmental practices. They are managed by professional fund managers who make the buying and selling decisions based on extensive research.

Compared to ETFs, mutual funds might offer less flexibility, as their shares can't be traded throughout the day. However, they can offer a more tailored approach to green investing, as they're often centered around specific themes or sectors within the sustainability field.

=== Green Mutual Funds – Weighing Risk and Return

Like all other investments, green mutual funds also come with risks. The portfolio's performance is tied to the financial health and business trajectory of the companies included in the fund. However, they can offer diversification benefits, possibly reducing risk.

On the returns side, their performance has been commendable in recent years, with many green mutual funds outperforming their conventional counterparts. Nevertheless, it's key to remember that past performance does not guarantee future results.

In conclusion, green bonds, ETFs, and mutual funds each hold substantial promise as green investment avenues. They come with their unique advantages and involve different risks, fitting differently into individual investors' profiles based on their financial goals, risk tolerance, and commitment to environmental sustainability. Therefore, deciding on the right mix hinges on thorough introspection and understanding of these instruments.

Consider consulting a financial advisor or investment specialist to guide your investment decisions and tread confidently into the world of green investing. Your financial aspirations and ecological values might find their harmonious meeting point as you help foster a greater good - a sustainable future!

Chapter 9. Risk Management in Green Investing: Be Informed, Be Safe

As we venture into the world of green investing, one cannot ignore the essence of risk management, the discipline that fortifies your financial decisions and paves the way for sustainable profits. In this chapter, we will cover various aspects such as identifying risks, opportunities, methods of managing and measuring risks, and a few practical tips to keep your investments safe.

9.1. Identifying Risks

Recognizing potential risks is the first step towards managing them. The risks involved in green investing can often be categorized into two main groups: financial risks and green risks.

Financial risks result from market volatility, liquidity issues, and other economic factors, just like any other conventional investment. Green risks, on the other hand, are related specifically to green investments. Examples include changes in environmental policies, technological advancements, and public perception towards green matters.

Investor education is key in identifying these risks. It involves staying updated about the global and local economic landscape, understanding the technologies involved, predicting how society might react to these technologies, and knowing the politics behind the environment regulations.

9.2. Opportunities

Understanding the global push for regulation and incentive measures to counter climate change can help identify opportunities in green investing. Governments and business organizations worldwide are increasingly becoming conscious about their roles in mitigating climate change. This growing awareness means more chances for growth in green industries.

Areas like renewable energy, smart power grid technology, waste management, and green buildings often provide excellent investment avenues. Always consider the long-term potential and scalability of these opportunities to ensure that your investment yields returns over time.

9.3. Measuring Risks

Comprehensively measuring risk is crucial to making informed investment decisions. Both qualitative and quantitative approaches are used for this purpose.

Qualitative assessments may involve evaluating the reputation of the company you're investing in. Their business practices, leadership, the predictability of their behavior, and how they respond to challenges can shed light on the company's resilience and integrity.

Quantitative analysis, meanwhile, uses statistical methods to understand and measure risk. This might include historical data analysis, scenario analysis, and financial modeling based on potential outcomes.

9.4. Managing Risks

Risk can't be entirely eliminated, but it can be mitigated and managed using a variety of strategies.

1. Diversification: Having a diverse portfolio helps to spread potential financial loss over a wide range of investments.

2. Research: Thorough research on companies, sectors, and market trends helps to better understand and anticipate risks.

3. Hedge: Hedging through derivatives or inverse ETFs can provide insurance against potential losses.

4. Timing: Being patient and investing long term often helps mitigate risks involved due to market volatility.

5. Regular Monitoring: Investments should be monitored regularly to take note of changes that might signal increased risk.

9.5. Practical Tips

Here are some practical tips to balance risk in your green investment portfolio:

1. Stay Updated: Follow the news and updates in the environmental sector to stay aware of latest trends and changes.

2. Network: Build a network of other green investors, join forums, or attend meetings to share and gain knowledge.

3. Get Expert Opinion: Seek advice from financial advisors who specialize in green investments.

4. Be Patient: Green investing sometimes requires patience, as real change takes time, and benefits might not be immediately visible.

In conclusion, while risk is an inherent part of any investment strategy, its management should be the cornerstone of your green investment strategy. Being thoroughly informed and adopting a safety-first approach will assist you in traversing the green investing landscape securely.

Chapter 10. Interviews with Global Leaders in Green Investing

It's heartening to note that the booming industry of green investing is being steered by a handful of passionate, sharp, and successful Global Leaders. To bolster our understanding of this sphere, we reached out to these pioneers. Their words will surely illuminate your path in this transformative journey!

10.1. Meeting the Maestro: Interview with Alice Anderson

Alice Anderson needs no introduction in the realm of green investing. The seasoned financial wizard currently helms Global Green Investments (GGI), a premier entity dealing with green bonds, green real estate, and ESG (Environmental, Social, and Governance) stocks.

When asked about her motivation to get into green investing, Alice shared that witnessing the damaging effects of climate change is what sparked the metamorphosis. She recalls, "It hit me: my financial skills could play a role in transforming environmental sustenance."

Alice recommends new investors begin with ESG-indexed funds, saying, "They offer stability, diversity and prove lucrative in the long run. Plus, they genuinely contribute to sustainability efforts."

10.2. Bridging Borders: Conversation with Diego Rodriguez

Diego Rodriguez, the maverick behind Ethical Wealth Partners, brought a fresh perspective to green investing from Latin America. Unsurprisingly, his focus areas are sustainable farming and renewable energy projects.

Diego's entry into this sector was incited by the rampant deforestation he observed in his native Brazil. "I knew I had to use my financial know-how to fight this. Green investing seemed obvious," he recounts.

Rodriguez advises, "For Latin America, specifically, sustainable agriculture investing is highly promising due to vast lands and consistent demand for organic produce."

10.3. Rewriting the Rules: Discussion with Haruki Tanaka

From the bustling metropolis of Tokyo, Haruki Tanaka joined our conversation series. The spirited CEO of Eco-Prospects Japan has been a game-changer, advocating for solar and wind energy industries.

Tanaka speaks of his initiation into green investing as one driven by necessity. "Japan's energy needs are immense; resorting to renewables was the only sustainable option," he opined.

His tip for budding green investors? "Renewable energy projects need investments and are very profitable. New technology adoptions like hydrogen fuel cells represent exciting opportunities."

10.4. Green from the Ground Up: Exchange with Fatima Zahra

Hailing from the vibrant subcontinent of India, Fatima Zahra's stance on green investing is slightly unconventional. This founder and CEO of Earth's Ally emphasizes green entrepreneurship with a niche focus on waste management and recycling startups.

"India was grappling with waste management issues, and I saw green startups devising innovative solutions. This had to be capitalized on," she explained.

Fatima highlight "Investing in green startups is risky but potentially rewarding. Look for innovative solutions addressing distinctly local environmental challenges."

10.5. Nurturing the Nordic: Interaction with Lars Eriksson

Our final conversation was with Lars Eriksson, a green investing giant from Sweden. Spearheading Green Finns, Eriksson has steered the focus towards water management projects, a crucial issue for the Nordic region.

"I've always been privy to the importance of water management, given our geography," he shared, adding, "We need investment in this increasingly critical sector."

Eriksson's tip for investors is to align with pressing regional environmental issues. "Look within your region for green investing opportunities; they may be closer than you think!"

Each of these industry stalwarts brings unique perspectives from their part of the globe. If one thing's clear though, it's that the opportunities in green investing are as vast and varied as the world itself. Alice, Diego, Haruki, Fatima, and Lars all harness their passions and expertise to make a difference, and their insights can serve as signposts on your personal journey towards responsible and rewarding green investing. Let them inspire you to make sound financial decisions that coincidentally, also have global impact! After all, your money can be a potent tool to forge a sustainable future.

Chapter 11. Future of Green Investing: Trends, Challenges, and Opportunities

Green investing is more than just following a trend; it's a method of aligning economic growth with environmental sustainability.

=== First, let's uncover what green investing means. It refers to the process of allocating funds into projects and companies that are committed to sustainable, socially responsible operations. These 'green' endeavours prioritize both their ecological footprint and their financial return.

11.1. The Rising Influence of Green Investing

In recent times, green investing has moved from the periphery to the mainstream investment landscape. The reason? Investor engagement with the effects of climate change, environmental degradation, and advents of responsible corporate behaviour. A clear shift in mentality is observable across the board, from individual investors to large corporations, underlining that profitability and sustainability are not mutually exclusive. UNEP FI reported a dramatic increase, from a few billion dollars in the 90s to almost $90 trillion in 2019. It's evident that green investing doesn't just contribute to a healthier planet—it also holds substantial financial promise.

11.2. Trends in Green Investing

Looking ahead, let's envision trends propelling market progression.

1. Increased Regulation: As governments worldwide intensify climate targets, businesses must make a strategic shift towards sustainable practices. This regulatory pressure is increasingly influencing public and private sector investments into renewable energy, eco-friendly technologies, and sustainable ventures.

2. Enhanced Transparency and Disclosure: An increasing push for transparency means companies need to disclose their environmental impact, making it crucial for them to invest in sustainable practices.

3. ESG Investing: The integration of Environmental, Social, and Governance (ESG) factors in investment decisions is becoming mainstream. It offers a robust lens to assess an organization's sustainability and ethical practices.

4. Preference for Sustainability: A growing trend among millennials and Generation Z investors is the shift towards eco-conscious investment—they prefer businesses that are upfront about their sustainability efforts.

5. Green Bonds: Emitting green bonds to fund renewable energy projects or other environmentally friendly initiatives will continue to be popular.

11.3. Challenges Encountered in Green Investing

Despite the promising growth, green investing faces some hurdles.

- Difficulty in Measuring Impact: There is no universal definition or standard to measure the 'greenness' of investments. The absence of a uniform criterion hampers comparability across investments.

- Greenwashing: Some companies exploit the rising demand for eco-conscious investments by misrepresenting their environmental impact, a deceptive practice known as greenwashing.

- High Entry Threshold: Some green sectors like renewable energy require significant initial capital investments, limiting participation.

11.4. Opportunities Ahead

So what does the future look like for green investing?

- New Markets and Innovation: As sustainable practices gain traction, there will be an emergence of new markets. Innovation will continue in areas like clean energy, circular economy, green transport, and sustainable agriculture.

- More Green Bonds: The increasing popularity of green bonds will provide new opportunities.

- Public-Private Partnerships: Raising public sector investment in collaboration with the private sector will accelerate green transformation.

- Green Finance Tools: We expect development in green financial tools and packages, garnering interest from retail investors.

11.5. Expert voices

In an interview, Mark Carney, UN Special Envoy for Climate Action and Finance, remarked, "Businesses that don't adapt, including companies in the financial system, will go bankrupt without question. US coal companies are a prime example."

On a similar note, Inger Andersen, Executive Director of UNEP, pointed out, "We have seen incredible growth in green financing recently, but the reality remains that we are still far from aligning with the goals of the Paris Agreement."

11.6. Conclusion

The pathway of green investing is undeniably riddled with challenges. Still, its future looks promising, and its role in driving environmental sustainability is indisputable. As we move towards green economies, green investing will serve as a critical lever.

Learning to navigate this evolving landscape, powered by this burgeoning demand for sustainability, will not only promise substantial returns but also the gratification that your investments are shaping a better world.

Remember, "The best time to plant a tree was 20 years ago. The second best time is now." So too, the best time to start green investing was 20 years ago, and the second-best time is now. So, let's get started!

www.ingramcontent.com/pod-product-compliance
Lightning Source LLC
Chambersburg PA
CBHW062307290526
45794CB00006B/2718